SPORTS TRACING FUN BOOK

by Joan Berger, Karen Braun, & Anita Sperling

Illustrated by Harry Trumbore

ISBN 0-590-42492-0

12 11 10 9 8 7 6 5 4 3 2 1   9/8 0 1 2 3 4/9
                Printed in the U.S.A.   11

First Scholastic printing, April 1989

SCHOLASTIC INC.

New York Toronto London Auckland Sydney

INSTRUCTIONS

Make up your own sports picture. Follow the instructions below.

1. Pick out your favorite sport and trace one of the bodies. Then add the legs.

2. Add a pair of arms from page 29.

3. Pick a face from page 28 and trace it onto the body.

4. Give the player the appropriate equipment for that sport from pages 30-31.

5. Keep on tracing players and equipment until you have arranged a "game" on the page. There are even stadiums full of people for you to trace!

Some Helpful Tips To Remember

1. Remember that by tilting the page when tracing legs or bodies, you can increase the number of "movement" possibilities open to you.

2. When adding equipment such as a mitt, it will be easier if you trace the arm without the hand—then you won't have to trace the mitt over another drawing.

3. Think about the entire picture you want to draw before you begin; that way you won't run out of space on the page before you've finished tracing.

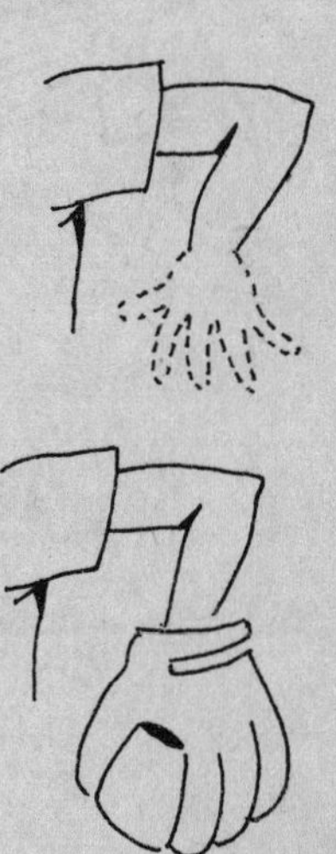

BASEBALL

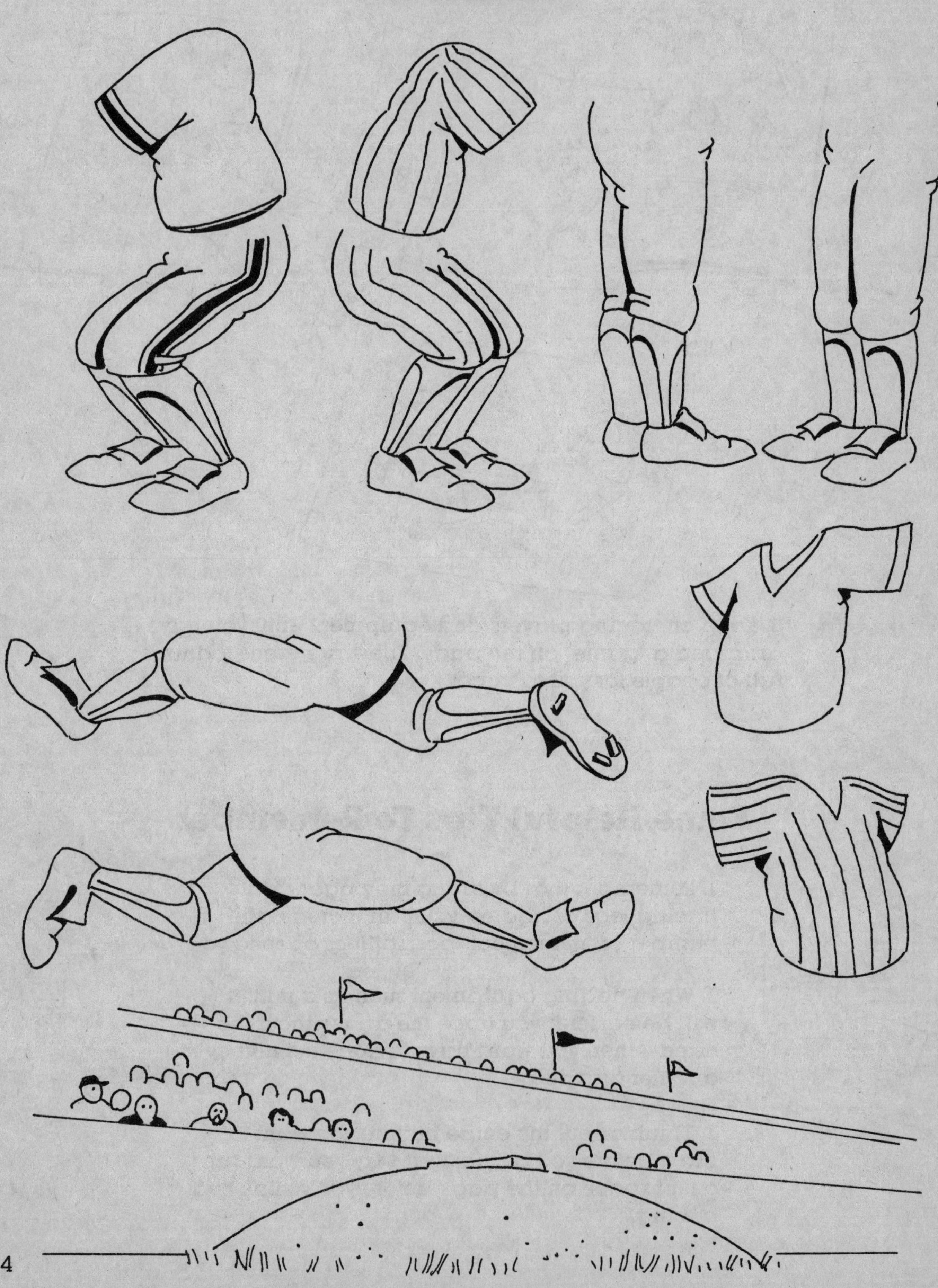

BASEBALL

1 2 3 4 5 6 7 8 9   R H E
HOME   0 0 0 1 0 1 2 0   4 3 0
VISITORS 0 0 0 0 1 0 0 0   1 0 1
BALL 2   STRIKE 2   OUT 1

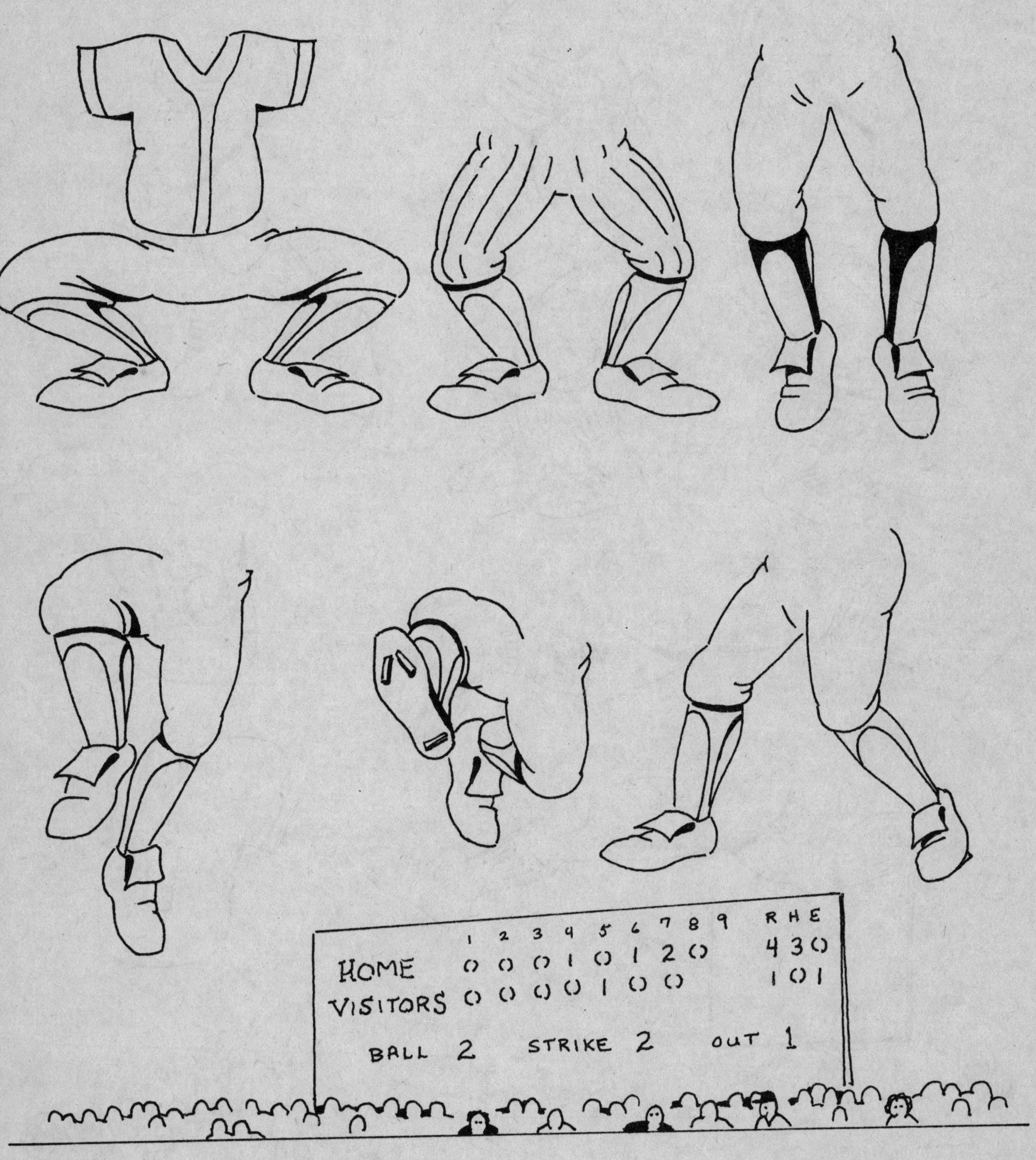

FOOTBALL

FOOTBALL

BASKETBALL

BASKETBALL

4
HOME VISITORS
68 72
QUARTER
00:43
HOME VISITORS
68 72
QUARTER
00:43

SOCCER

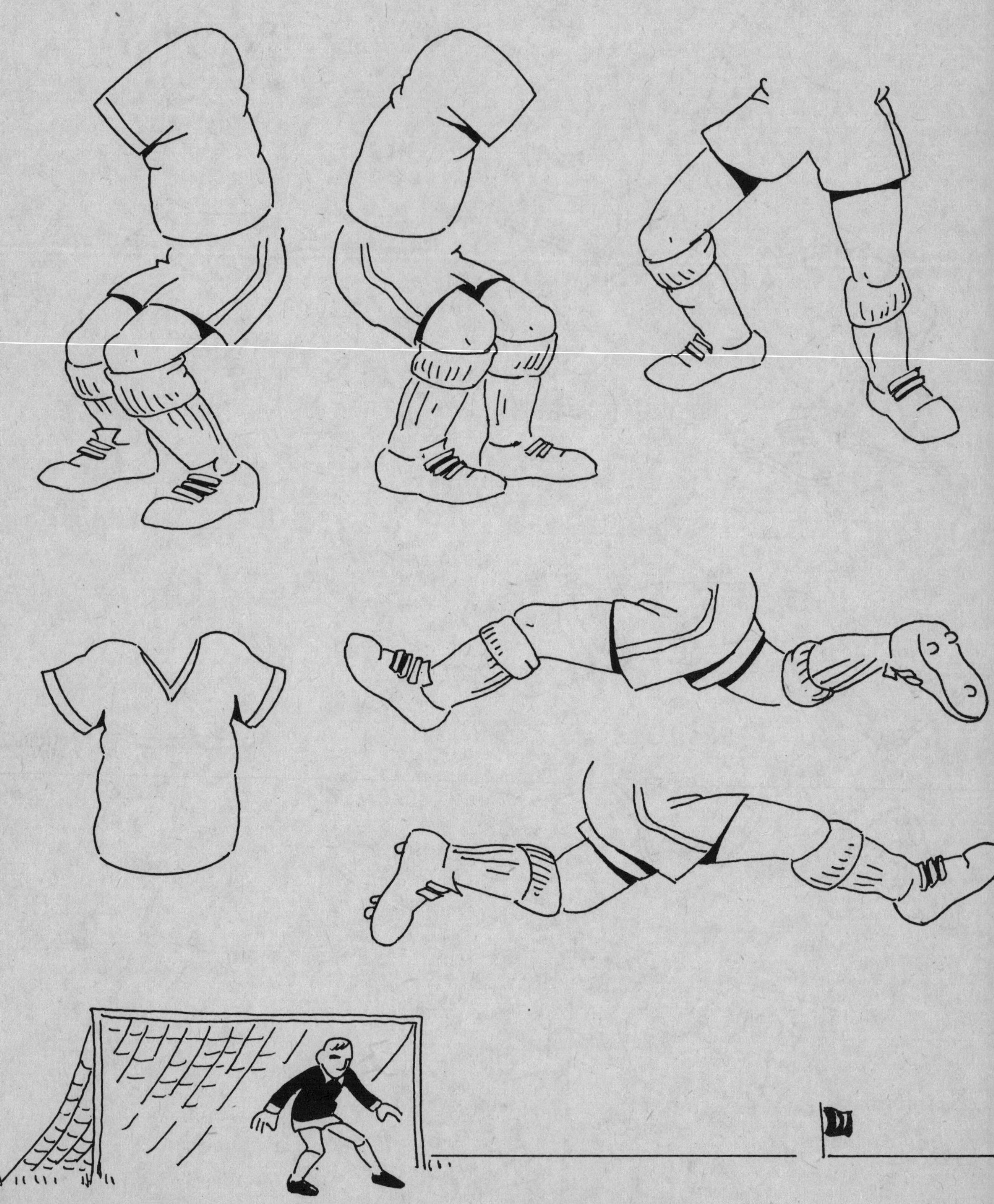

SOCCER

FACES

ARMS

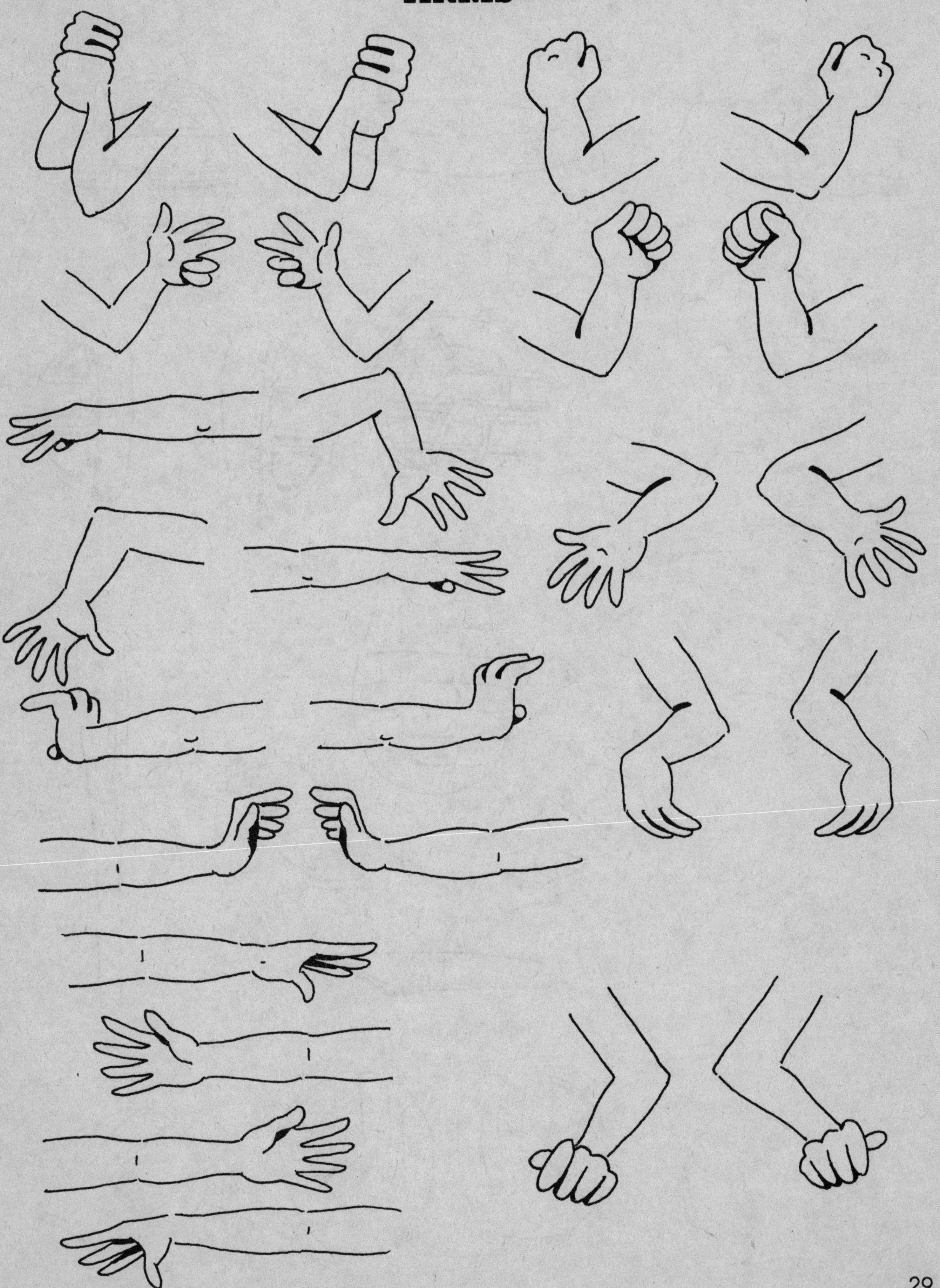

EQUIPMENT

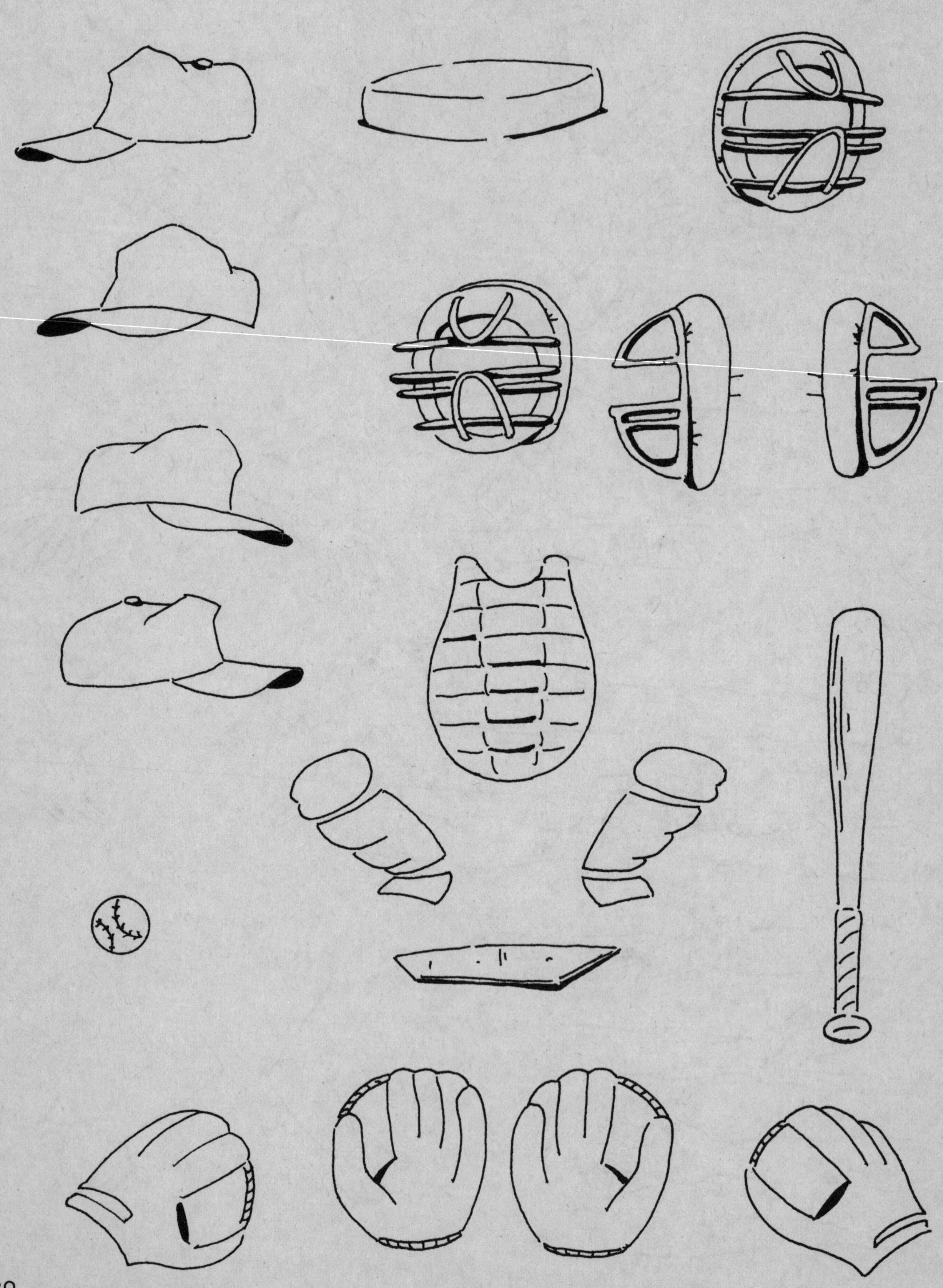

EQUIPMENT

EXAMPLES